How Many Cookies Do You Have?

one

two

three

four

five

six

seven

eight

How many cookies do you have?

I have one cookie.

How many cookies do you have?

I have two cookies.

How many cookies do you have?

I have three cookies.

How many cookies do you have?

I have four cookies.

How many cookies do you have?

I have five cookies.

How many cookies do you have?

I have six cookies.

Let's learn about France.

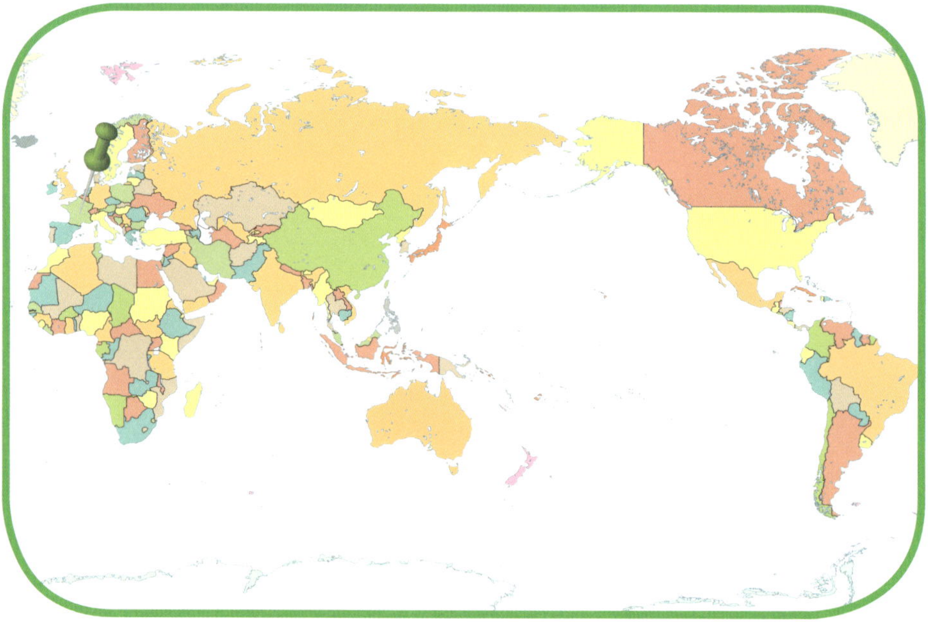

Flag of France

Eiffel Tower